Snakes
Slither and Hiss

DK Penguin Random House

Written by Fiona Lock
Series Editor Deborah Lock
U.S. Editor John Searcy
Art Editor Mary Sandberg
Production Editor Siu Chan
Production Pip Insley
Jacket Designer Martin Wilson

Reading Consultant
Linda Gambrell, Ph.D.

First American Edition, 2008, 2012
This edition, 2015
Published in the United States by DK Publishing
345 Hudson Street, New York, New York 10014

15 16 17 18 19 10 9 8 7 6 5 4 3 2 1
001—271118—June/15

A catalog record for this book is available
from the Library of Congress.

ISBN: 978-1-4654-3504-0 (Paperback)
ISBN: 978-1-4654-3505-7 (Hardcover)

DK books are available at special discounts when purchased in bulk for sales promotions,
premiums, fund-raising, or educational use. For details, contact:
DK Publishing Special Markets
345 Hudson Street, New York, New York 10014
SpecialSales@dk.com

Printed and bound in China

The publisher would like to thank the following for their kind permission to reproduce their photographs:
(Key: a=above, b=below/bottom, c=center, l=left, r=right, t=top)
1 PunchStock: Design Pics. **4 Dorling Kindersley:** Jerry Young (tr, c, cl). **4–5 Dorling Kindersley:** Jerry Young (b).
5 Dorling Kindersley: Jerry Young (br). **8–9 naturepl.com:** Mary McDonald. **9 NHPA / Photoshot:** James Carmichael Jr (
10–11 Science Photo Library: David M. Schleser / Nature's Images. **12 Alamy Images:** Image Quest Marine/Justin
Peach (br). **12–13 naturepl.com:** Pete Oxford. **14–15 NHPA / Photoshot:** Image Quest 3-D. **15 NHPA / Photoshot:**
Daniel Heuclin (t). **16 FLPA:** Michael & Patricia Fogden/Minden Pictures (br). **17 Corbis:** Rod Patterson/Gallo Images.
18–19 Science Photo Library: S. R. Maglione. **22–23 Alamy Images:** Michael Moxter/Vario Images Gmbh & Co.kg.
24 naturepl.com: Luiz Claudio Marigo. **25 Corbis:** Ralph Clevenger (tr). Jake Socha: (c). **26–27 Photolibrary:** Mauritiu
Die Bildagentur Gmbh. **26 naturepl.com:** Tony Phelps (c). **28 Alamy Images:** Dan Sullivan (cl). **Dorling Kindersley:** Jerr
Young (fbl). **naturepl.com:** Geoff Simpson (cra). **Photolibrary:** Animals Animals/Earth Scenes (cb). **29 Photolibrary:**
Animals Animals/Earth Scenes (cb). Specialist Stock: Martin Harvey (t). **30 naturepl.com:** Mary McDonald (bl); Pete
Oxford (cla). **Photolibrary:** Alastair Shay (cl). Inside back cover: **NHPA / Photoshot:** Image Quest 3-D.
Jacket images: Front: **Corbis:** Joe McDonald. Back: **Science Photo Library (SPL):**
David M. Schleser / Nature's Images (cra).
All other images © Dorling Kindersley
For further information see: www.dkimages.com

A WORLD OF IDEAS:
SEE ALL THERE IS TO KNOW

www.dk.com

Contents

Hiss!

See the scaly snakes
slither here and there.

scales

Rat snakes

egg

This baby rat snake
slides out of its egg.

Hiss!

Copperheads

Look out!
This copperhead flicks
its tongue in and out.

Hiss!

tongue

Parrot snakes

Look out!
This parrot snake opens
its jaws wider and wider.

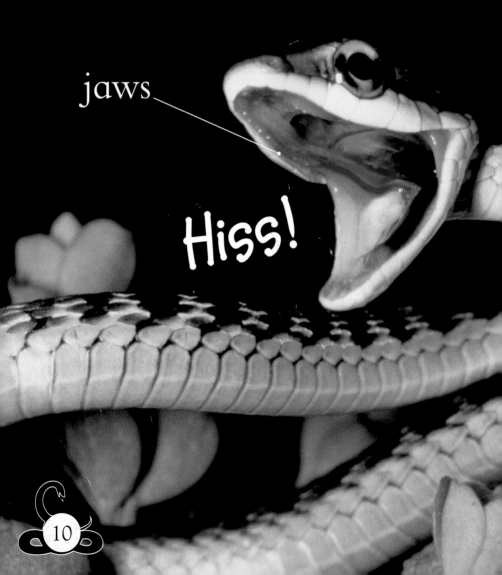

jaws

Hiss!

Pit vipers

Look out!
This pit viper bites
with its sharp fangs.

fang

Hiss!

Rattlesnakes

Look out!
This rattlesnake
rattles its tail when
it is angry.

tail ——————

Rattle!

Cobras

hood

Look out!
This cobra is getting
ready to spit.

Sssspit!

Pythons

Look out!
This python wraps
around a rat and
squeezes tight.

Sssqueeze

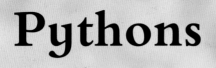

rat

Gaboon vipers

Look out!
This gaboon viper
hides in the leaves.

Ssssh!

leaves

snake

Sea snakes

Look out!
This sea snake swims
this way and that.

Ssswish!

stripes

Flying tree snakes

Look out!
This flying tree snake
glides from branch to
branch.

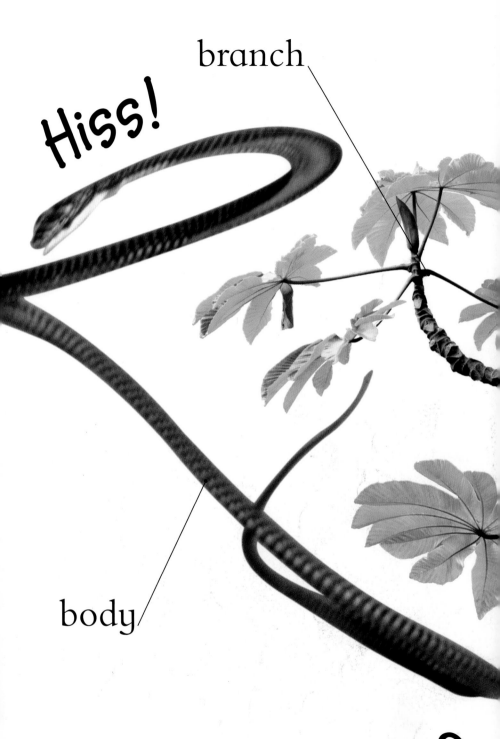

branch

Hiss!

body

Horned vipers

Look out!
This horned viper
winds its way
across the sand.

Hiss!

trail

sand

27

See the sleepy snakes
curl up in coils.

Ssssh!

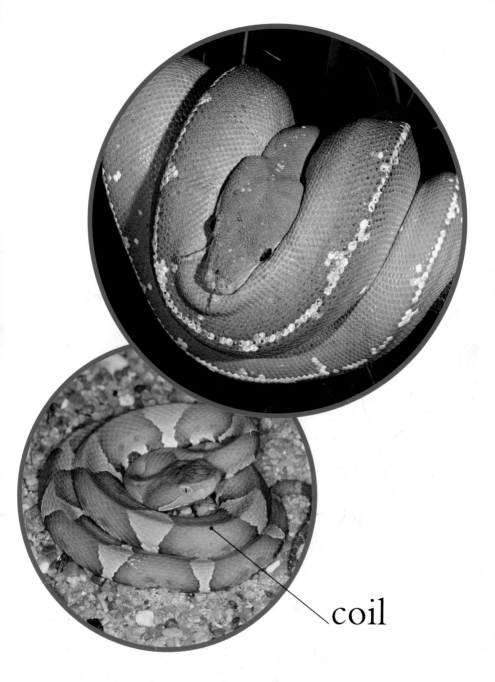

coil

Can you slither
and hiss like a snake?

Glossary

Egg
a soft, leathery shell with a baby snake growing inside

Fang
a large hollow tooth that shoots out poison

Jaws
bones that open and close the mouth

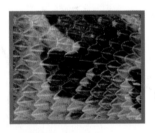

Scales
small, smooth plates that cover the skin

Tongue
a mouth part that can smell, touch, and taste

Index

Have you read these other great books from DK?

LEARNING TO READ

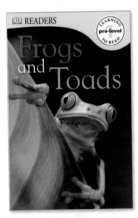

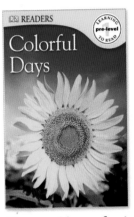

Croak! Move in closer to look at the frogs and toads of the world!

Chatter! Meet the monkeys as they scamper, climb, and jump.

Play and have fun! Enjoy the colorful days throughout the year.

BEGINNING TO READ

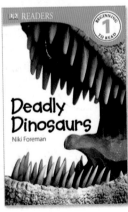

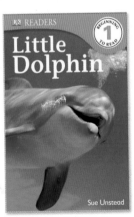

Roar! Thud! Meet the dinosaurs. Who do you think is the deadliest?

Click! Whistle! Join Little Dolphin on his first ocean adventure alone.

Hard hats on! Watch the busy machines build a new school.